# The Year of the Poet VII

## June 2020

**The Poetry Posse**

*inner child press, ltd.*

# The Poetry Posse 2020

Gail Weston Shazor
Shareef Abdur Rasheed
Teresa E. Gallion
hülya n. yılmaz
Kimberly Burnham
Tzemin Ition Tsai
Elizabeth Esguerra Castillo
Jackie Davis Allen
Joe Paire
Caroline 'Ceri' Nazareno
Ashok K. Bhargava
Alicja Maria Kuberska
Swapna Behera
Albert 'Infinite' Carrasco
Eliza Segiet
William S. Peters, Sr.

~ * ~

In order to maintain each poet's authentic voice, this volume has not undergone the scrutiny of editing. Please take time to indulge each contributor for their own creativity and aspirations to convey their uniqueness.

hülya n. yılmaz, Ph.D.
Director of Editing ~
Inner Child Press International

# General Information

## The Year of the Poet VII
**June 2020 Edition**

## The Poetry Posse

**1st Edition : 2020**

This Publishing is protected under Copyright Law as a "Collection". All rights for all submissions are retained by the Individual Author and or Artist. No part of this Publishing may be Reproduced, Transferred in any manner without the prior **WRITTEN CONSENT** of the "Material Owners" or its Representative Inner Child Press. Any such violation infringes upon the Creative and Intellectual Property of the Owner pursuant to International and Federal Copyright Laws. Any queries pertaining to this "Collection" should be addressed to Publisher of Record.

**Publisher Information**
**1st Edition : Inner Child Press**
intouch@innerchildpress.com
www.innerchildpress.com

This Collection is protected under U.S. and International Copyright Laws

Copyright © 2020 : The Poetry Posse

ISBN-13 : 978-1-952081-20-0 (inner child press, ltd.)

$ 12.99

WHAT WOULD LIFE BE WITHOUT A LITTLE POETRY?

# Dedication

This Book is dedicated to

## *Humanity, Peace & Poetry*

the Power of the Pen

can effectuate change!

&

The Poetry Posse

past, present & future

our Patrons and Readers

the Spirit of our Everlasting Muse

*In the darkness of my life  
I heard the music  
I danced...  
and the Light appeared  
and I dance*

Janet P. Caldwell

# Table of Contents

*Foreword* ......... ix

*Preface* ......... xiii

*Albert John Lutuli* ......... xvii

# The Poetry Posse

| | |
|---|---|
| Gail Weston Shazor | 1 |
| Alicja Maria Kuberska | 9 |
| Jackie Davis Allen | 15 |
| Tezmin Ition Tsai | 21 |
| Shareef Abdur – Rasheed | 27 |
| Kimberly Burnham | 33 |
| Elizabeth Esguerra Castillo | 39 |
| Joe Paire | 45 |
| hülya n. yılmaz | 51 |
| Teresa E. Gallion | 57 |

# Table of Contents ... *continued*

| | |
|---|---|
| Ashok K. Bhargava | 63 |
| Caroline Nazareno-Gabis | 69 |
| Swapna Behera | 75 |
| Albert Carassco | 81 |
| Eliza Segiet | 87 |
| William S. Peters, Sr. | 93 |

## June's Featured Poets — 103

| | |
|---|---|
| Eftichia Kapardeli | 105 |
| Hussein Habasch | 113 |
| Kosh K Mathew | 119 |
| Metin Cengiz | 125 |

## Inner Child News — 133

## Other Anthological Works — 161

# Foreword

We talked of information explosion in the late 1980s, the information superhighways through the 1990s. We are so much engrossed to leave our digital foot prints today but the Greater Peace is always hash tagged with love, humanity and core values.

"Peace is the loaf of bread for a beggar
the first monsoon for a farmer
a butterfly on the mast of a submarine
five elements of a creation
seven notes of music"

Peace is a journey and never a destination. So, in the process of learning to inculcate inner peace in our lives we search, research and recognise the values. The perception of peace is different for different people.

This month's theme was dedicated to Noble Peace laureate Albert John Luthuli, also spelled as Lutuli. He was a Zulu chief, religious leader, teacher, and president of the African National Congress (ANC), South Africa. He became the first African to be honoured with the prestigious Nobel Prize for Peace in 1960 for his leadership role in non-violent struggle against the apartheid rule in South Africa. He had a noble bearing, and was intolerant of hatred, and firmly struggled for equality and peace among all men of the South African society. He was awarded the Nobel Peace prize for advocating non-violent resistance against apartheid in South Africa. In leading his people, he was always democratic and consulted his people before any decision taken. He was honest, transparent and accountable to his people.

In his acceptance speech he said "May the day come soon. when the people of the world will rouse themselves, and together effectively stamp out any threat to peace in whatever quarter of the world it may be found,"

The Inner Child Press with its mission of building bridges of cultural understanding takes the responsibility for global peace and harmony through poetry with International Anthologies. We respect the great peace leaders, the land, nature, folk tales, culture, music, literature, perceptions, ideas, thoughts, language and all ethnic groups of the world.

Literature has undergone a tectonic change. We express our deep reverence to all the noble peace laureates for they are the apostles of a time zone who have solved the situations, saved human lives and helped the economic, cultural social growth of society. The Year of the Poet has dedicated each month of 2020 to the noble peace laureates.

Poetry is the living song of human race ........

We respect the humanity ...
We respect history and coexistence
Let us join our hands for peace and build a
paradise on the Earth ...

Swapna Behera

Cultural Ambassador of India and South East Asia
for Inner Child Press International

# World Healing World Peace 2020

## Poets for Humanity

*Now Available*

www.innerchildpress.com/world-healing-world-peace-poetry

www.worldhealingworldpeacepoetry.com

www.worldhealingworldpeacefoundation.org

# Preface

Dear Family and Friends,

Yes I am excited and feel accomplished as we enter our seventh year of publishing what I and many others deem to be a worthy enterprise, *The Year of the Poet*.

This past year we have aligned our vision with that of Nober Peace Prize Recipients. We have title this year's theme. The Year of Peace! Hopefully thorugh our sharing each month, our poetry can have a profound effect on our global consciousness and the need for peace while educating ourselves and our readership about some of the individuals who have made history through their efforts to promulgate peace for all of humanity.. We are on our way to hitting yet another milestone. Needless to say, I am elated.

To reiterate, our initial vision was to just perform at this level for the year of 2014. Since that time we have had the blessed opportunity to include many other wonderful poets, word artists and storytellers in the Poetry Posse from lands, cultures and persuasions all over the world. We have featured hundreds of additional poets, thereby introducing their poetic offerings to our vast global audience.

In keeping with our effort and vision to expand the awareness of poets from all walks by making this offerings accessible, we at Inner Child Press International will continue to make every volume a FREE Download. The books are also available for purchase at the affordable cost of $7.00 per volume.

In the previous years, our monthly themes were Flowers, Birds, Gemstones, Trees and Past Cultures. This coming year we have elected to continue our focus of choosing what we consider a significant subject . . . PEACE! In each month's volume you will have the opportunity to not only read at least one poem themed by our Poetry Posse members about such celebrated Peace Ambassadors, but we have included a few words about each individual in our prologue. We hope you find the poetic offerings insightful as we use our poetic form to relay to you what we too have learned through our research in making our offering available to you, our readership.

In closing, we would like to thank you for being an integral part of our amazing journey.

Enjoy our amazing featured poets . . . they are amazing!

*Building Cultural Bridges of Understanding . . .*

Bless Up . . . From the home in our hearts to yours

*Bill*

The Poetry Posse
Inner Child Press Ineternational

PS

Do Not forget about the World Healing, World Peace Poetry effort.

Available here

www.worldhealingworldpeacepoetry.com

**For Free Downloads of Previous Issues of
The Year of the Poet**

www.innerchildpress.com/the-year-of-the-poet

# World Healing, World Peace Foundation
*human beings for humanity*

worldhealingworldpeacefoundation.org

# Albert John Lutuli
# 1960

Each month for the year of 2020, which we have deemed as *The Year of Peace*, we at Inner Child Press International will be celebrating through our poetry a few Nobel Peace Prize Recipients who have contributed greatly to humanity via their particular avocations. This month of June 2020 you will find select poems from each Poetry Posse member on this month's celebrants.

In 1960, The Nobel Peace Prize was awarded to Albert John Lutuli.


For more information about visit :

en.wikipedia.org/wiki/Albert_Lutuli
or
www.nobelprize.org/prizes/peace/1960/lutuli/biographical

Poets . . .
sowing seeds in the
Conscious Garden of Life,
that those who have yet to come
may enjoy the Flowers.

Poets, Writers . . . know that we are the enchanting magicians that nourishes the seeds of dreams and thoughts . . . it is our words that entice the hearts and minds of others to believe there is something grand about the possibilities that life has to offer and our words tease it forth into action . . . for you are the Poet, the Writer to whom the Gift of Words has been entrusted . . .

~ wsp

*poetry is . . .*

*Poetry succeeds where instruction fails.*

*~ wsp*

Gail Weston Shazor

# Gail Weston Shazor

This is a creative promise ~ my pen will speak to and for the world. Enamored with letters and respectful of their power, I have been writing for most of my life. A mother, daughter, sister and grandmother I give what I have been given, greatfilledly.

Author of . . .

"An Overstanding of an Imperfect Love"
&
Notes from the Blue Roof

Lies My Grandfathers Told Me

available at Inner Child Press.

www.facebook.com/gailwestonshazor
www.innerchildpress.com/gail-weston-shazor
navypoet1@gmail.com

## Continuous Rain

Mvumbi accidently taught the world
That to be black was accidental
He accidently stood easy
When there was great need
To be accidently found non-violent
In a world where his accidentiality
Was considered passive
They thought it an accident that
The Christianity didn't take
And he reverted to tribal chief
As Mvumbi missioned his purpose
The ancestral voices came forth
Too loud to be mistaken
And the ones who insisted he was Albert
Pushed back against the nations
Until an accident occurred
And the Zulu's mourned.

## Re-Breath

I listen to you breathe
And I am awed by your easy peace
The relaxed shoulders of one
Who dreams big and quiet
"Mom, tell me a story"
And it comes forth in memories and wishes
The colors are grand
The words, in a hurry for the saying
Driving the point home
Driving the story to God
The lesson pressing towards love
The cords fray from navel to wrist
With the wearing of time
In the loudness of living you laugh
Choosing a blessing over bitterness
And how is it be known
What is truth and what is fancy
The lesson is this
Don't cry because it ends
Laugh because it is happening
I watch you from my end of the day
The seasons pass far too quickly
And the hours grow thin
As time changes from yesterday
Into the wonder of tomorrows
The meanings change
In the turnings
We have wound around each other
From living to begin
To living to end

# Gail Weston Shazor

We carry in turn our hearts
I watch you breathe
And count the moments
We spend together
I have asked for my story
From the inhalation
May you ask for mine
At exhalation
As you watch them breathe

## The Art Forbidden
*Song of Solomon*
*3:1-3*
*By night on my bed I sought him whom my soul loveth: I sought him, but I found him not. I will rise now, and go about the city in the streets, and in the broad ways I will seek him whom my soul loveth: I sought him, but I found him not. The watchmen that go about the city found me: to whom I said, Saw ye him whom my soul loveth?*

Why did you hide from me
I beseeched you earnestly
In city streets and
Lanes paved wide
Across heaven's horizons
I sought your face
My soul longed for you
Every watchman watched
But none could help me
Find you who I desired
Above the touch of strangers
That I will always shun
By night I dreamed
Of your sweet voice
Calling out to me
Calling me from evensong
In the quietest hour
Twixt now and then
Though in all faith
I prayed without ceasing
I fasted on my knees
I called you by name

But you answered not
Your essence still lingers
Around every memory
Those that keep count
Of us who are alone
Cannot erase the stain of tears
As there is no grace
Sufficient to make an art
Of being one forbidden love

# Alicja Maria Kuberska

# Alicja Maria Kuberska

Alicja Maria Kuberska – awarded Polish poetess, novelist, journalist, editor. She was born in 1960, in Świebodzin, Poland. She now lives in Inowrocław, Poland.

In 2011 she published her first volume of poems entitled: "The Glass Reality". Her second volume "Analysis of Feelings", was published in 2012. The third collection "Moments" was published in English in 2014, both in Poland and in the USA. In 2014, she also published the novel - "Virtual roses" and volume of poems "On the border of dream". Next year her volume entitled "Girl in the Mirror" was published in the UK and "Love me" , " (Not )my poem" in the USA. In 2015 she also edited anthology entitled "The Other Side of the Screen".

In 2016 she edited two volumes: "Taste of Love" (USA), "Thief of Dreams" ( Poland) and international anthology entitled " Love is like Air" (USA). In 2017 she published volume entitled "View from the window" (Poland). She also edits series of anthologies entitled "Metaphor of Contemporary" (Poland)

Her poems have been published in numerous anthologies and magazines in Poland, the USA, the UK, Albania, Belgium, Chile, Spain, Israel, Canada, India, Italy, Uzbekistan, Czech Republic, South Korea and Australia. She was a featured poet of New Mirage Journal ( USA) in the summer of 2011.

Alicja Kuberska is a member of the Polish Writers Associations in Warsaw, Poland and IWA Bogdani, Albania. She is also a member of directors' board of Soflay Literature Foundation.

## Evening in Africa
*poem dedicated to Albert John Lutuli*

Dark clouds whirl like bad moments.
They obscure the setting sun
and the bloody glow closes the day.

This moment gives a birth to my reflection
- the calm of the evening is disturbed by a storm,
and a man destroys the harmony of the world
Another and long chapter in human history
described the power and enormity of the empire
and contempt for the black color of the skin.

Suddenly a ray breaks through the clouds
a luminous spark gives comfort and hope
when it paints a rainbow on the raindrops

Not so long ago a boy was born,
who was sensitive to pain of a man,
He called evil by name bravely.
His words sounded like new music.
Freed thoughts gave independence
and crushed the megalith of injustice.

Africa stands proudly upright now.
It wiped the tears of suffering for slaves
and again looks boldly into the future.

## Come back of everyday life

It will be fine again
and the world
will regain its brilliance.
Time will go on,
bad hours will pass
- these ones filled with fear,
suffering and tears.
One day the death will forget
to sharpen its scythe.

Joy will return home
to bloom on the faces
Sadness and fear
will settle in memories
like a bit of dust
- only sometimes
they will echo in the nightmare dreams
or will recall in the stories
about long days of horror

## Your name

You said:
„ A man - it sounds proudly"
and you mean
Einstain, Mozart or Rafaello

Later you added:
"A man- it sounds terribly"
and you mean
Hitler, Stalin or Pol Pot

Now, you must choose your way.
You have to decide
if your name makes people
smile or cry.

# Jackie Davis Allen

# Jackie Davis Allen

Jackie Davis Allen, otherwise known as Jacqueline D. Allen or Jackie Allen, grew up in the Cumberland Mountains of Appalachia. As the next eldest daughter of a coal miner father and a stay at home mother, she was the first in her family to attend and graduate from college. Her siblings, in their own right, are accomplished, though she is the only one, to date, that has discovered the gift of writing.

Graduating from Radford University, with a Bachelors of Science degree in Early Education, she taught in both public and private schools. For over a decade she taught private art classes to children both in her home and at a local Art and Framing Shop where she also sold her original soft sculptured Victorian dolls and original christening gowns.

She resides in northern Virginia with her husband, taking much needed get-aways to their mountain home near the Blue Ridge Mountains, a place that evokes memories of days spent growing up in the Appalachian Mountains.

A lover of hats, she has worn many. Following marriage to her college sweetheart, and as wife, mother, grandmother, teacher, tutor, artist, writer, poet and crafter, she is a lover of art and antiques, surrounding herself, always, with books, seeking to learn more.

In 2015 she authored *Looking for Rainbows, Poetry, Prose and Art*, and in 2017, *Dark Side of the Moon*. Both books of mostly narrative poetry were published by Inner Child Press and were edited by hulya n. yilmaz.

in 2019, No Illusions.Through the Looking Glass, which was nominated to be considered for a Pulitzer Prize by the publisher and editor of InnerChild Press, ltd.

http://www.innerchildpress.com/jackie-davis-allen.php
jackiedavisallen.com

Jackie Davis Allen

## Continuous Rain: His Zulu Name

Albert Mvumbi John Luthuli,
Servanthood of justice.
Activist, inspired by Gandhi.
With passionate heart and soul,
Resisted against apartheid, always engaged.
Continuous rain: Mvumbi.
That was his Zulu Name

Albert Mvumbi John Luthuli, teacher,
Politician, chief. A Zulu,
South African, caring son.
Guided by Christian principles.
Confirmed Methodist, lay pastor.
Continuous Rain: Mvumbi.
That was his Zulu Name

Albert Mvumbi John Luthuli,
Banned, restricted, though
Unrelenting in his goal for racial equality.
Eloquently negotiating with whites;
Stripped from his role as tribal chief.
Continuous Rain: Mvumbi.
That was his Zulu Name

Albert Mvumbi John Luthuli,
Impeccable morals, character.
Traveled to India, the United States of America.
Awarded the 1960 Nobel Peace Prize:
First African so honored.
Continuous Rain: Mvumbi.
That was his preferred name.

## About Love's Name

There was a time
when we were not yet hardened.
Earth, too, in its newly formed garden.
So much fun when embraced in the romance
of love's warm arms.

Love danced the bright light of desire's charm!

The music, fidelity's commitment.
How it blossomed.
Blush of astonishment!
And the turtledoves,
how sweetly they cooed.

Why, then, did dark clouds choose to descend?

They rained down in such way
that the sun withheld its light.
Love, passion, dissolved
into guile's potion,
tainting love's name.

Pleasure's cup of emotion wept.

Like storm of discontent
regret shamed their hearts.
With innocence of trust torn apart,
how, you may ask, can love's name
ever be the cause of blame?

## A Version of the Truth

Stand by the shore, look out at the sea, and
Somberly, heart is sinking in grief, scarred
Beyond relief. Why is it that some see what
Others don't want to see, and why is it that
They don't understand how truth views life?

The sound, the world overflowing, its banks
Brimming fully with wealth, knowledge and truth.
Alas, had truth's version been able to drink
Of its blessings, it may have allowed one to navigate
The path to its borders, to cross over the bridge.

Barred by tradition, universal misunderstanding.
There, where the current swells, where deeply
Hidden, the secret treasures enjoyed by elders,
Love would have been like a fountain, springing
Forth and uniting truth's family in affection

Alas, it was not to be for the recipients whose
Foreign ways clashed with the stringent
Tenets of the old regular ways of religion.
The budding of romance, the stems clipped.
The formation of the leafing out of passion, faded..

O, that truth's version surfaced, had it not been forbidden.
One class pitted against another, though color
Of skin, remarkably the same. Either in light of
Day or dark of night. Alas, the cast of blame paints
In black and white the stains of truth's alternative name.

# Tzemin Ition Tsai

# Tzemin Ition Tsai

Dr. Tzemin Ition Tsai (蔡澤民博士) was born in Republic of China, in 1957. He holds a Ph.D. in Chemical Engineering and two Masters of Science in Applied Mathematics and Chemical Engineering. He is a professor at Asia University (Taiwan), editor of "Reading, Writing and Teaching" academic text. He also writes the long-term columns for Chinese Language Monthly in Taiwan.

He is a scholar with a wide range of expertise, while maintaining a common and positive interest in science, engineering and literature member. He is also an editor of "Reading, Writing and Teaching" academic text and a columnist for *'Chinese Language Monthly'* in Taiwan

He has won many national literary awards. His literary works have been anthologized and published in books, journals, and newspapers in more than 40 countries and have been translated into more than a dozen languages.

## Let The Rain Continue

As the east wind blows
Willow's silk dance
Those anti-Apartheid activists
The only black Africans with deprived voting rights
Discriminatory laws
Like the pond water quietly waiting for the stormy storm
full of ponds
Must not extinguish
The lone lamp in the center of the lotus pond
Would rather let the rain continue

Grass on the plain
The moisture of the dew has just dried up
Bans
Following the Sharpeville massacre
Lie on the empty bed, listening to the rain from the south
window
Who can't sleep by night lights
The Nobel Peace Prize ceremonies in Oslo
An inexplicable pathological phenomenon

Willow trees on the lake covered with white flowers
In the smoke, unable to overcome its weights and hang
down everywhere
Let the rain continue
Circular shore
Pedestrian figure seems to be in the fog on spring evening
When the snow on a sunny day warms the wind
The quiet mood will naturally become clearer

## Thoughts of my life knew before

The page full poems
The thoughts full night
Just for that heartbreak
Just for so many past memories crowded in upon my mind
Teared up the poem page
I suddenly lost the page of thought

The page full poems
The completely torn night
Did not see the so-called peace of mind
My mind has been hollowed out
Conceived the poem
Also broke off the lingering night

Carefully posted back a page
The torn scar
Scotch tape fall to pieces
As if
The bandages for healing
Smooth it out daily
Still can't wait for the recovered soul
How can I
Not blame
my selfishness?

## Life and Death In The Forest

Look at this fruit as bright red as blood, it will not just be a dream in our forest
If you want to
Snatch
Between you and me
There won't be only wails

Among these vast forests, would not just conceive only one fruit like this
Had better not dare to try anything
Extinguish
That greed in your eyes
Or blood red will not only contaminate the fruit

Your claws are not as sharp as mine
Your beak is not as hard as me
Your wings and feathers are less plump than me
Your will is not as firm as mine
Your voice even is not as sad as mine

Under my scalding, ruthless eyes
This red
It's already hot as flames, crimson like fires
Not afraid of getting yourself under the fire
Bring it on

Shareef Abdur Rasheed

# Shareef Abdur Rasheed

Shareef Abdur-Rasheed, AKA Zakir Flo was born and raised in Brooklyn, New York. His education includes Brooklyn College, Suffolk County Community College and Makkah, Saudi Arabia. He is a Veteran of the Viet Nam era, where in 1969 he reverted to his now reverently embraced Islamic Faith. He is very active in the Islamic community and beyond with his teachings, activism and his humanity.

Shareef's spiritual expression comes through the persona of "Zakir Flo" . Zakir is Arabic for "To remind". Never silent, Shareef Abdur-Rasheed is always dropping science, love, consciousness and signs of the time in rhyme.

Shareef is the Patriarch of the Abdur-Rasheed Family with 9 Children (6 Sons and 3 Daughters) and 41 Grandchildren (24 Boys and 17 Girls).

For more information about Shareef, visit his personal FaceBook Page at :

https://www.facebook.com/shareef.abdurrasheed1
https://zakirflo.wordpress.com

## Albert Lutuli..,
----------------
b. 1898
d.
Zulu chieftain
teacher
respected
man of peace
relentless
seeking justice
abolish apartheid
in South Africa
persecuted for
ANC activism
from 1945
one of early leadership
Mandela contemporary
withstood sustained
restricted movement
banned from freedom
to travel
peaceful resistance
against apartheid
Nobel peace prize
recipient 1960
one of the soldiers
for justice who are
willing to sacrifice
their lives in peaceful
resistance.
his sacrifice left its mark
in the long struggle
against inhuman racist
tyranny in South Africa


food4thouight = education

## X-cited!!
*Dedicated to brother Malcolm, AL Hajj Malik(ra)*

X-ception since conception!
X-Tracted, May 19,1925!
X-posed to racist deception
X-celled at trying to stay alive
X-tremely gifted inside
X-ample of the guided strive
X-acted so the oppressed are lifted
X-pressed what's needed to survive
X-ponent of speaking truth to might
X-pounded on Human rights
X-Fought the good fight, it's fact alright
X-hounded by the Alphabet guys day and night
X-ported far all the way to Hajj for real not a mirage
X-horted "No one's worthy of worship X-cept Allah!"
X-treme sacrifice to the day he died
X-traordinary one sent to lead
X-cellent brother Al-Hajj Malik Shabazz, Shaheed, (ra)
X-pired Feb. 21 1965 but i,
X-pect to Insha'Allah be with him one day!!
Remember they (Martyrs) are not dead,
You just don't see them, instead!!


food4thought = education

## Rabil Alamin
*Lord of the Worlds*
-------------------

got the whole joint
locked down
including dem self-anoint
dem think wear crowns
dem clowns
datz da point
ya'll delusional
since mortality
is the usual
tenure brief
can't rule from where
dem lay reefs
nuff said bout kings speak
none of ya'll
have power of ' Be '
fact:
be and it is to be exact
only Allah(swt) does that
and right now it's on
delusional clowns reduced
to pawns reminded who's
the boss
ceeee
to degree only his biz
only thee (1) say be and it is


food4thought = education
(swt) = All glory to Allah.

# Kimberly Burnham

# Kimberly Burnham

A brain health expert with a PhD in Integrative Medicine, Kimberly Burnham has lived in tropical Colombia; in Belgium during the Vietnam War; in Japan teaching businessmen English; in diverse international Toronto, Canada and several places in the US. Now, she's in Spokane, WA with her wife, Elizabeth, two sets of twins (age 11 & 14) and three dogs. Her recent book, *Awakenings: Peace Dictionary, Language and the Mind, a Daily Brain Health Program* includes the word for peace in hundreds of languages. Kim's poetry weaves through 70 volumes of *The Year of the Poet, Inspired by Gandhi, Women Building the World, A Woman's Place in the Dictionary*, Tiferet Journal, Human/Kind Journal and more.

https://www.nervewhisperer.solutions/
https://www.linkedin.com/in/kimberlyburnham/

## Human Rights On The Agenda

A Nobel Peace Prize sends a message
inspired by Mahatma Gandhi
South African chief
teacher and trade unionist
Albert Lutuli earned the Prize in 1961
the committee took a stand
respect for human rights on the agenda
joining the movement against apartheid.
honoring civil disobedience
directed against racial segregation
then took a step further in 1984
respecting South Africa's Bishop Desmond Tutu
with the award

## Values in a Motto

Lesotho has a motto
showing what we value
"Khotso Pula Nala"
Peace Rain Prosperity

We say these words
as if prayers
for what we don't have

Hoping for the best days in Marakabei
when all three come together
folding into a graceful life

Two hundred sheep
ten goats thirty cattle and five horses
all together we enjoy a life of "Khotso"
with "Pula" creating "Nala"

## Peace Talking and Telling Tales

"The most loquacious people"
J. Marshall observed
referring to the Ju/'hoan
suggests one useful strategy
maintaining peace "fgou"
diffusing tensions by talking
the San people of the Kalahari Desert
are not silent "fgau"
engage in conversation
all day long and well into the night
as they work
as they eat
as they gather around the fires
with their children at night
as they visit with other families
people who have hunted or gathered separately
recount in exhaustive detail
the tracks of animals
amounts of berries
abundance of certain plants
then plan what come next
where might there be game?
to whom will they give nuts?
the band a unit of sharing
demands peace and cooperation among members

# Elizabeth E. Castillo

# Elizabeth Esguerra Castillo

Elizabeth Esguerra Castillo is a multi-awarded and an Internationally-Published Contemporary Author/Poet and a Professional Writer / Creative Writer / Feature Writer / Journalist / Travel Writer from the Philippines. She has 2 published books, "Seasons of Emotions" (UK) and "Inner Reflections of the Muse", (USA). Elizabeth is also a co-author to more than 60 international anthologies in the USA, Canada, UK, Romania, India. She is a Contributing Editor of Inner Child Magazine, USA and an Advisory Board Member of Reflection Magazine, an international literary magazine. She is a member of the American Authors Association (AAA) and PEN International.

## Web links:

Facebook Fan Page

https://free.facebook.com/ElizabethEsguerraCastillo

Google Plus

https://plus.google.com/u/0/+ElizabethCastillo

## Of Peace and Rain

Blessed with a name of continuous rain,
Mvumbi, a lover of peace
First person of African Heritage
To have the Nobel Peace Prize
Struggled for non-violent means
Against apartheid.

The Zulu Chief who laid his life
For his pack of ten million,
He once said: "You must learn the rules of the game,
And then you have to play better than anyone else."

Peace and rain, a lovely refrain,
Harmony and unity will remain
A noble man of peace
Set the world in bliss.

## The Sojourner

In my search for meaning-
I often wondered where is my place in this world,
Scanning the skies in a moonlit night
Marvelling at the cosmic chaos, the blinding light
Glancing at the eddies-
The vast universe before me full of questions,
And the answers are yet to surface
The sojourner lost in oblivion
Hiding behind the shadows
Waiting for years of revelation
About to take step in the next chapter of the millennium,
With eyes wide open, soul in deep reflection
The embers start to ignite
And yet the restless heart suddenly crashed and burned.

Greeted by the mystic twilight,
Asking the heavens for a Divine Guide-
The Sage said: "the answers will come to you."
That's the mystery of my own fragility,
A stranger with no home, a vagabond on the street of life
But deep in my heart I know
My Personal Legend will reveal itself in time-
Like a thief in the night, it will come to me in a dream
And then I'll be lost no more
The wanderer metamorphosed into a Divine Soul.

## And They Healed

Restless souls pleading to the heavens,
Surrounded by angels, harps playing
The skies of blue greeted them anew
Leaves of green like palms outstretched,
As if succumbing to a fervent prayer.

Prisoners of their own doing,
Leading solitary confinement
When will they see the breaking of a new dawn?
Masked faces enveloped in fear and scorn.

Frightened of the darkness,
Weary shadows, creased faces
The Promise etched in the sands of time,
God will hear their cries.

Waking up to a brand new morn,
They can never go back to what they were once
The Plague being a catalyst to change,
Repent they did, and they healed.

Light from the heavens emerged,
The glaring rays of the sun
Creating a vibrational shift
Man realized his faults and mistakes,
And they healed.

# Joe Paire

# Joe Paire

Joseph L Paire' aka Joe DaVerbal Minddancer . . .
is a quiet man, born in a time where civil liberties were a walk on thin ice. He's been a victim of his own shyness often sidelined in his own quest for love. He became the observer, charting life's path. Taking note of the why, people do what they do. His writings oft times strike a cord with the dormant strings of the reader. His pen the rosined bow drawn across the mind. He comes full-frontal or in the subtlest way, always expressing in a way that stimulate the senses.

www.facebook.com/joe.minddancer

## Africa's First

Peace doesn't come easy when one fights for human rights
Albert John Lutuli found that out in life as with most of his countrymen
Ah the country men, like Bishop Desmond Tutu
that a fight for peace is a righteous fight
Albert John Lutuli, born 30 November 1897
Can you imagine what was happening during his lifetime
when the country where he was born in needed a lifeline
Apartheid comes to mind, demonstrations and strikes
against a minority government
He went on to be elected President
of the African National Congress, liberation movement
Following a massacre of 69 black demonstrators
in Sharpeville the ANC was banned
This man was persecuted by his own authorities
A South African chief, a teacher and trade unionist
A spokesmen for a campaign of civil disobedience
There's so much more to this storied poem
as we struggle to keep his struggle from becoming a norm
His Nobel Peace Prize for 1960, lifts me spiritually
Bulawayo, Southern Rhodesia (now Zimbabwe)
His country His land his demand for justice
Minority rule? Is the definition of injustice.

## Lost In Thought

I've found myself wandering and losing tract of time
it's not the first time but as of late, man wow
I woke up Monday only to be aware Wednesday
Tuesday I guess I must have been thinking

I know I'd been drinking while watching the blues
that's my personal definition of watching the news
No time to worry about time I have no time
I have no place I need to be, just be

What to me, as having fun isn't how it used to be
I'm free of worrying about being late
and being late used to be a pet peeve
I believe my hobbies are avoiding me

I have a stereo that's incredibly old
it's no longer hooked up
umm, give away or sold
I told you I'm lost in thought

I thought if I taught a class but alas
I have no patience for patients
seems a bit too salacious
how can I say this, yeah! Lost in thought

## Joe Paire

## Reopening The Same

Refried, re-tried, we tried to get back to normalcy
We seem to have forgotten who moves the economy
Opening stores without the patrons
how can we economically restore a nation
The brothers are on lockdown
The others are on lockdown
The people are being knocked down
Empty streets empty venues
Empty policies with nothing but innuendo
the death toll is rising
the government is lying
PEOPLE ARE DYING but money matters more
The CEO's are sore; they can't capitalize like before
Liquor stores are essential to help dull your mental
Now remind us again what's essential
Restaurant dates your favorite teams
Let's go back to patrons you know, "WE THE PEOPLE"
We're the ones who actually keep you high and mighty
neat and tidy, fed and well read, so answer politely
Why are we opening up so soon, when the death toll
still looms without an answer to this doom
Are we not men or are we chess pieces
moved about based on their thesis, their prophecies?
There hunches, people are literally dying in bunches
economists elaborately crunch their numbers
Have we all becomes victims of war
when there's more on the front line like with wars before
Buyer beware, we're off of protection
We're merely numbers to crunch for a bottom line at
"HELL'S END"

# hülya n. yılmaz

# hülya n. yılmaz

Liberal Arts Emerita, hülya n. yılmaz is a published author, literary translator, and Co-Chair and Director of Editing Services at Inner Child Press International. Her poetic work appeared in an excess of eighty-five anthologies of global endeavors and has been presented at numerous national and international poetry events. In 2018, the Writer's International Network of British Colombia, Canada honored yılmaz with a literary award. As of 2017, two of her poems remain permanently installed in *Telepoem Booth* – a U.S.-wide poetic art exhibition. hülya finds it vital for everyone to understand a deeper sense of self, and writes creatively to attain a comprehensive awareness for and development of our humanity.

Writing Web Site
https://hulyanyilmaz.com/

Editing Web Site
https://hulyasfreelancing.com

## Honorable Albert John Luthuli

the moment your smile met my eyes
from a photo from the Nobel Foundation archives,
your graceful dignity spoke to my heart distinctly

Honorable Albert John Luthuli,
you already know, but i am finding out just now
so, i hope you will bear with me
while i tell myself and willing others
a few details about this segment of your life

your initiatives and actions for peace on Earth
were acknowledged with a Nobel Peace Prize
the year was 1960

Honorable Albert John Luthuli,
you received the distinctive award one year later
during that time, the designated committee
also decorated Dag Hammarskjöld
with the same honor
posthumously

Honorable Albert John Luthuli,
Africa's first Peace Prize Laureate
a distinguished leader of global peace
what a privilege it has been for me
to learn about your exceptional existence
beyond the death of your empirical presence!

you have exemplified respect for human rights
while you were filled with inner strength
to fight against apartheid
draped inside the philosophy
of nonviolence

Honorable Albert John Luthuli
in how much of a dire need are we of you
in our indisputably troubled times!

## a HAIKU on peace

i despair, i do!

the world is suffocating

under evil's chains

hülya n. yılmaz

## Africa's First Peace Prize Laureate

he is said to have traversed the Earth about 69 years
Inkosi Albert John Luthuli, as far as his on-paper-identity
but also known under his Shona name, Myumbi

as a teacher and an activist of South Africa
he opened his door to the political arena
the year was 1952, and peace is where he took the people to

be proud, Africa, be very proud!
you have birthed an exceptional soul
i wish and wish again against all odds
that the rest of the world would follow suit
i have had it with the games of the cruel!

# Teresa E. Gallion

# Teresa E. Gallion

Teresa E. Gallion was born in Shreveport, Louisiana and moved to Illinois at the age of 15. She completed her undergraduate training at the University of Illinois Chicago and received her master's degree in Psychology from Bowling Green State University in Ohio. She retired from New Mexico state government in 2012.

She moved to New Mexico in 1987. While writing sporadically for many years, in 1998 she started reading her work in the local Albuquerque poetry community. She has been a featured reader at local coffee houses, bookstores, art galleries, museums, libraries, Outpost Performance Space, the Route 66 Festival in 2001 and the State of Oklahoma's Poetry Festival in Cheyenne, Oklahoma in 2004. She occasionally hosts an open mic.

Teresa's work is published in numerous Journals and anthologies. She has two CDs: *On the Wings of the Wind* and *Poems from Chasing Light*. She has published three books: *Walking Sacred Ground, Contemplation in the High Desert* and *Chasing Light*.

*Chasing Light* was a finalist in the 2013 New Mexico/Arizona Book Awards.

The surreal high desert landscape and her personal spiritual journey influence the writing of this Albuquerque poet. When she is not writing, she is committed to hiking the enchanted landscapes of New Mexico. You may preview her work at

*http://bit.ly/1aIVPNq* or *http://bit.ly/13IMLGh*

## Albert Luthuli Impact

Luthuli was a charitable man, intolerant of hatred
and persistent in his work for equality and peace.
Tribal Chief and president-general of the
African National Congress, a leader in nonviolent
campaigns for civil rights in South Africa.

The government placed bans on Luthuli's
movement because of his work. After one ban
expired in 1956, he attended an ANC conference
was arrested and charged with treason. He was
eventually released and charges dropped.

Another five-year ban confined him to a 15-mile radius
of his home. The ban was temporarily lifted for 10 days
to permit Luthuli to attend the Nobel ceremony.

He was awarded the Nobel Peace Prize
for his role in the non-violent struggle
against apartheid bringing more widespread
attention to segregation in South Africa.

## What Do We Fear

What do we fear most when
we step into the day?

A chance encounter with the hounds
that hold our guilt and shame.
They may sit at our table and
feast on our pain.

Or perhaps we may have to own
the deadly words
that beat the bed of tears
our friend shed.

Or perhaps it is the face of grief
in the stranger's eyes that
mirror the sorrows we stuff
in our closet.

Shall we analyze our pain
on the sharp blade of our tongues
one slice at a time?

Or shall we move on to face
the fear that we must pass
to step into our next life.

Teresa E. Gallion

## Turning Point

Enormous cold clutches my heals,
climbs up my legs,
freezes me in place.
I send heat waves of love.
My legs move away from the cold.

The voice of a tragic relationship
runs up my spine,
paralyzes my body.
I relax and let go.
The voice melts in the wind.

A broken shadow stands in my lane
blocking my passage.
I throw a pure kiss of love
into its face.
The shadow falls off my path.

The face of lust staggers behind me
reaching for my tail.
I drop rose petals on my footprints.
Lust dissolves into a stream of love.

I walk alone on my trail,
come face to face with fear.
It reaches for me with bloody hands.
I touch the hand of fear
with the light of love.
Fear turns into my spiritual guide.

# Ashok K. Bhargava

# Ashok K. Bhargava

Ashok Bhargava is a poet, writer, community activist, public speaker, management consultant and a keen photographer. Based in Vancouver, he has published several collections of his poems: Riding the Tide, Mirror of Dreams, A Kernel of Truth, Skipping Stones, Half Open Door and Lost in the Morning Calm. His poetry has been published in various literary magazines and anthologies.

Ashok is a Poet Laureate and poet ambassador to Japan, Korea and India. He is founder of WIN: Writers International Network Canada. Its main objective is to inspire, encourage, promote and recognize writers of diverse genres, artists and community leaders. He has received many accolades including Nehru Humanitarian Award for his leadership of Writers International Network Canada, Poets without Borders Peace Award for his journeys across the globe to celebrate peace and to create alliances with poets, and Kalidasa Award for creative writings.

## Glide Upstream

*life gives unto life*
*you, the giver*
*and you, receiver*
*rise together on the gift*
*as on wings* – Khalil Gibran

live in harmony
be a bold greenhorn

peace begins with you
it ends with you

float upstream
be a giver to receiver it forever

rise as on wings
land on delicate petals

only in the service of others
to find a meaningful peace

the best way to have peace
is to be peaceful


*Om Shanti, the ancient hymn has long been used as one of the mantras longing peace for the humans, the universe, and the whole cosmic manifestation. It serves as a prayer for peaceful coexistence.*

## Change is Hope

Salt water becomes sweet
when transformed into a cloud.

A crater becomes a pristine lake
after hot magma escape.

Flower becomes fragrance
when touched by the breeze.

Silence becomes sunshine
in the unbearable blues of quarantine.

Soul reemerges
when body turns into ash.

Why can't we see
beauty of the change?

Life must flame out
to give new light

to guide a cocoon
from a moth to a butterfly.

## Letter to a Friend

I am sad
I cannot sleep
I am blue
and I want to weep.

I am abandoned by
the relatives and family
I have no lover to help me
in a calamity.

They envy my job
reputation and pay
they blame me for their troubles
now what can I say.

I think I should leave everything
without hesitation
to attain happiness
and liberation.

Can you confirm
aptness of my decision
that detachment is the answer
in precision?

Caroline
'Ceri Naz'
Nazareno
Gabis

# Carolin 'Ceri' Nazareno-Gabis

Caroline 'Ceri Naz' Nazareno-Gabis, World Poetry Canada International Director to Philippines is known as a 'poet of peace and friendship', a multi-awarded poet, editor, journalist, speaker, linguist, educator, peace and women's advocate. She believes that learning other's language and culture is a doorway to wisdom.

Among her poetic belts include 7 th Prize Winner in the 19 th and 20 th Italian Award of Literary Festival; Writers International Network-Canada "Amazing Poet 2015", The Frang Bardhi Literary Prize 2014 (Albania), the sair-gazeteci or Poet Journalist Award 2014 (Tuzla, Istanbul, Turkey) and World Poetry Empowered Poet 2013 (Vancouver, Canada). She's a featured member of Association of Women's Rights and Development (AWID), The Poetry Posse, Galaktika Poetike, Asia Pacific Writers and Translators (APWT ), Axlepino and Anacbanua.

Her poetry and children's stories have been featured in different anthologies and magazines worldwide.

Links to her works:

panitikan.ph/2018/03/30/caroline-nazareno-gabis
apwriters.org/author/ceri_naz
www.aveviajera.org/nacionesunidasdelasletras/id1181.html

## His Name Is Liberation
*For Albert John Lutuli*

you are a crossbreed
of thoughts, ideas,
knowledge and freedom,
in a multi-stage
of higher creative and reasonable thinking
if "ego" is not the absolute value
it will create harmless bitterness,
you remain calm, just, humble and sincere,
the emergence of selfless acceptance,
you see more rooms of trying,
to liberate oneself from
discrimination and rejection
 even your character has been
killed many times,
you'd see things beyond structure
and beyond new sprouts
you are called laureate for peace—
a full grown hybrid of wisdom.

## Seed of Change

the colossal growth

of each vision

is coming together

as one seed of CHANGE,

remain steadfast

amidst contagion,

as Nature bloom,

we rise for tomorrow

while making heartprints

to those we know

and we don't know.

## whispered silence

i am nowhere
nameless born free dragonfly
 dressing my found wings
with my optimistic sun
holding new and old hours
of embryonic flames

i am where i would like to
host of outnumbered stars
in  the timeless sky
where rainbows bleed
within my flight
to reach you

i am just around here
your most gentle wind
of unspoken vermilion rings
here-there of now, for us
i am everywhere, in every you
 my love, like there's no tomorrow

# Swapna Behera

# Swapna Behera

Swapna Behera is a bilingual contemporary poet, author, translator and editor from Odisha, India. She was a teacher from 1984 to 2015. Her stories, poems and articles are widely published in National and International journals, and ezines, and are translated into different national and International languages. She has penned six books. She is the recipient of the Prestigious International Mother Language UGADI AWARD WINNER 2019. She was conferred upon the Prestigious International Poesis Award of Honor at the 2nd Bharat Award for Literature as Jury in 2015, The Enchanting Muse Award in India World Poetree Festival 2017, World Icon of Peace Award in 2017, and the Pentasi B World Fellow Poet in 2017. She is the recipient of Gold Cross of Wisdom Award, the Prolific Poetess Award, The Life time Achievement Award, The Best Planner Award, The Sahitya Shiromani Award, ATAL BIHARI BAJPAYEE AWARD 2018, Ambassador De Literature Award 2018, Global Literature Guardian Award, International Life Time Achievement Award and the Master of Creative Impulse Award. She has received the Honoured Poet of India from the Seychelles Government accredited Literary Society LLSF. Her one poem A NIGHT IN THE REFUGEE CAMP is translated into 50 languages. She is the Ambassador of Humanity by Hafrikan Prince Art World Africa 2018 and an official member of World Nation's Writers Union, Kazakhstan 2018. Italy, the National President for India by Hispanomundial Union of Writers (UHE), Peru, the administrator of several poetic groups, and the Cultural Ambassador for India and south Asia of Inner Child Press U.S.

Swapna Behera

## almost everyday .....

almost everyday
I enter into the fire to melt ;
to bleed and sweat
alphabets hop on my fossil

I reinvent my inner space
sprouting the blisters
wonderfully invading presumptions and assumptions
I become an orphan bagpiper
I chase the silence

almost everyday
my story and history barricaded
I try to speak unspoken dialects
I walk on the national highways
as a migrant labourer
hungry and thirsty
yet
dreaming my courtyard with hazy eyes
the murmuring sound of my village stream
echoes in my ears
I swim in hallucination ;
build my imaginary house with a strong roof
that can withstand disasters

almost everyday
I dig a well to drink water
but then who cares....?
I die to live and let you live .....

## autograph......

be assured my autograph
you are present
here or there ;somewhere

to allure the melody of my grinning soul
my skeleton squeezed in the captive land
why should I cry ?

every land has its own fragrance
each pollen grain can cross your boundaries
each dust particle has enormous dialogues
perfect rhythm loves dignity and democracy
invisible metaphors explode

be assured my darling autograph
you are the ray of hope
you are still living under the national flag
you are the ceremony of a journey
you survive in every buffer zone
on grass blades

yes, dear autograph
your silence is the anthem
in every language
be assured ......
love is in the air ...

## all about a peacemaker

a zulu leader he was
in a distant village of southern Rhodesia
who knew how to protest
a teacher, a preacher, and passionate educator
his dreams were for his own people
his heart cried for they were treated differently
had no access for education or health
the humiliation ,the policy of no rights to vote
a visible battle against apartheid he fought
with non violence
for he knew
love is more powerful a weapon
and stronger than hatred.
collectively they raised the voice
a winner he was
a noble peace laureate
Albert Luthuli
we remember you
today ,tomorrow and forever

# Albert 'Infinite' Carrasco

# Albert 'Infinite' Carassco

Albert "Infinite The Poet" Carrasco is an urban poet, mentor and public speaker.

Albert believes his experience of growing up in poverty, dealing with drugs and witnessing murder over and over were lessons learnt, in order to gain knowledge to teach. Albert's harsh reality and honesty is a powerfully packed punch delivered through rhyme. Infinite grew up in the east part of the Bronx and still resides there, so he knows many young men will follow the same dark path he followed looking for change. The life of crime should never be an option to being poor but it is, very often.

Infinite poetry @lulu.com

Alcarrasco2 on YouTube

Infinite the poet on reverbnation

## Infinite Poetry

http://www.lulu.com/us/en/shop/al-infinite-carrasco/infinite-poetry/paperback/product-21040240.html

## Albert Lutuli

Born in 1893, Died in 1967
The Nobel peace prize of 1960 went to Albert John Luthuli,
Otherwise known as Mvumbi.
Albert Luthuli was born in Rhodesia,
Which is now Zimbabwe in South Africa.
Mr Luthuli wasn't just a Nobel winner,
He was an activist, a politician as well as a teacher.
In 1933 Albert was asked to be chief of a Zulu tribe that were Christian,
Two years later he became a chieftain.
In 1952 Albert was elected to be president of the African National Congress,
He continued serving until 1967, the year of his accidental death.
Albert Luthuli was devoted to turning tides of apartheid.
The government arrested him for no reason and claimed he committed treason,
Almost a year later he continued his movement after being released from prison.
Before Albert Luthuli returned to the essence,
South Africa felt his humble presence.

## Before I take a sip

I don't drink often but when I do I pour out a bit for those that R.I.P before I take a sip. Salud my kin. Infinite went from the bricks to cages, from the bricks to stages, from the bricks to pages, been going thru it leveling up makn power moves, ya know boss life phases.

I'm always going to rep my genre hard like a body when it's soul returns to the father... I've always been around gangsters, drugs and guns growing up in a hood where parks were full of chalk marks outlining a murder. The only people out we're hustlers, killers, fiends and undercovers, I walked on shells of all calibers, needles with blood all over, old stems clogged with cut/baking soda and caps of all colors, got caught up young and left my mark like crayola, the block knows what is, bust everything from hands to shoulder stocks and went thru the entire spectrum... Roy G Biv. There's a million ways to die, if ya crossed me in these housing developments you'll be the million and one experiment. Had to stay alive by any means necessary whether it's a jagged edge or a pointy tip you're gonna get done dirty, don't start none won't be none, all I was doing was trying to get out of poverty by stacking my money to get out the slums.

# Covid-19

Our bodies are under attack, some are home self quarantined, others are in icu praying for that miracle vaccine. There's a Red Cross naval ship, tents, buildings and warehouses filled with beds for the sick, because hospitals are packed and there's not enough space for newest covid-19 patient's to fit. Without bullets flying by and bombs bursting in the air healthcare workers are seeing flatline after flatline like our soldiers see during wartime. I've spoken to a lot of doctors and nurses, their tears run down their faces as they try to paint pictures of what they're seeing. Al so many are coming in and not leaving, respiratory organs are failing causing patients to stop breathing. Family and friends can't visit to try to prevent the spread of covid, so before they flatline healthcare workers are letting them use their phones to say final bye's through FaceTime. Rest In Peace to all that couldn't pull through, blessings to all the survivors... Infinite is now one too

# Eliza Segiet

Eliza Segiet - A graduate of Jagiellonian University, The author of poetry volumes. *Romans z sobą* [*Romance with Oneself*] (2013), *Myślne miraże* [*Mental Mirages*](2014), *Chmurność* [*Cloudiness*] (2016), *Magnetyczni* (2018) *Magnetic People-* translation published in The USA in 2018, *Nieparzyści* [*Unpaired* ] (2019), A monodrama *Prześwity* [*Clearance*] (2015), a farce *Tandem* [*Tandem*] (2017), Mini novel *Bezgłośni* [*Voiceless*](2019 ). Her poems can be found in numerous anthologies both in Poland and abroad. She is a member of The Association of Polish Writers and The World Nations Writers Union. The laureate of The International Annual Publication of 2017 for the poem Questions, and for the Sea of Mist in Spillwords Press in 2018. For her volume of Magnetic People she won a literary award of a Golden Rose named after Jaroslaw Zielinski (Poland 2019 r.). Her poem The *Sea of Mists* was chosen as one of the best amidst the hundred best poems of 2018 by International Poetry Press Publication Canada. In The 2019 Poet's Yearbook, as the author of *Sea of Mists*, she was awarded with the prestigious Elite Writer's Status Award as one of the best poets of 2019 (July 2019).

She was awarded *World Poetic Star Award* by World Nations Writers Union – the world's largest Writers' Union from Kazakhstan (August 2019).
In September 2019 she was 1st Place Laureate (Foreign Poetry category) – in Contest *Quando È la Vita ad Invitare* for poem *Be Yourself* (Italy).
Her poem *Order* from volume *Unpaired* was selected as one of the 100 best poems of 2019 in International Poetry Press Publications (Canada).
In November 2019 she is a nominee for Pushcart Prize.

## Brethren
*In memory of Albert John Luthuli*
*Nobel Peace Prize laureate for 1960*

He objected to racial segregation,
violence, persecutions.

He knew,
that if anywhere in the world
were people oppressed,
there wouldn't be peace.

Reaching a hand out
towards a Human
means more than
aggression or hatred.
Not skin color,
but respect
should unite people.

It's love towards brethren
that permits survival.


*Translated by Ula de B*

## Human Tragedy

A cry for nothing,
everyone nearby became deaf.
No one can hear calls for help!
Nobody wants to hear anymore!
Who else can react?

Only a watchful rat
who emerges from his burrow
to taste human hatred!


*Translated by Artur Komoter*

## Hallucinations

I do not remember myself from yesterday.
Maybe some demon swirled in the mind?
Maybe
the past of those such as I
does not exist at all?

We were created
to hide our origin
from serial killers.
And at night
– hidden
in the moonlight
we feed ourselves with hallucinations.

*Translated by Artur Komoter*

# William S. Peters Sr.

# William S. Peters, Sr.

Bill's writing career spans a period of over 50 years. Being first Published in 1972, Bill has since went on to Author in excess of 50 additional Volumes of Poetry, Short Stories, etc., expressing his thoughts on matters of the Heart, Spirit, Consciousness and Humanity. His primary focus is that of Love, Peace and Understanding!

Bill says . . .

I have always likened Life to that of a Garden. So, for me, Life is simply about the Seeds we Sow and Nourish. All things we "Think and Do", will "Be" Cause and eventually manifest itself to being an "Effect" within our own personal "Existences" and "Experiences" . . . whether it be Fruit, Flowers, Weeds or Barren Landscapes! Bill highly regards the Fruits of his Labor and wishes that everyone would thus go on to plant "Lovely" Seeds on "Good Ground" in their own Gardens of Life!

to connect with Bill, he is all things Inner Child

www.iaminnerchild.com

Personal Web Site

www.iamjustbill.com

## For you Albert John Lutuli

From the land where Kings and Queens,
Chieftains and Griots
Are borne naturally,
Passing through the halls
Where generations of soul
Are taught,
Cultivated,
That they may become learned
In the ways
Of the 'au-naturale' man
There came he,
A man of reason,
A man of peace . . .
Albert John Lutul

It was not an easy road to travel,
When there was so much occupation
By those who transplanted themselves
To gather the riches
Of the indigenous man's lands

Still he searched for a way,
A resolution
To establish
A peaceful co-existence,
But parity of the equity
Was, as it still is
An elusive impish conundrum . . .
Still he strived

Yes, he had to strive . . .
That's right, STRIVE
For Civil Rights
In his own land.
Swallow his innate pride
Of being a noble independent African
To seek a peace
That would protect his people
From the racist bias
That infected the homeland

Because he chose a peaceful way
Instead of the outright
Purging,
Bloodletting
Of the lesser populace,
The greater populace
Of the European
Recognized him
With a prize  . .
a Nobel Peace Prize.

They call that 'Civility'

## Silence no longer cries

The 'Sound of Silence'
Has changed the color
Of its clothing . . .

It is no longer cloaked
In the solemn hues
Of greys and blues
That whispers compassion
And understanding

For many years
It waited
With an anxious patience
Waiting,
Waiting
For the pendulum to swing
Back,
Back
And balance this mechanism
We call
Humanity,
Civility,
And Righteousness
With a blind integrity
That was
All inclusive . . .
It did not

So, the silence
Went to the closet
And dressed itself
In blaring, flaring

Reds and oranges
Denoting the fury
That was allowed to manifest
Amongst us

Unrest,
Is never civil
When it
Involves
What we have devolved to
In the seeking of justification,
And answers
As to what is wrong
When we unjustifiably wrong
Those who are doing no wrong
Except in the delusional perspectives
Of the few
Who seem to like
To operate
On the wrong side
Of that delusional history book
That is filled with
Mis-truths,
Incomplete truths,
And lies

Herein belies the problem
And trust me if you will,
As we continue
With the blood-letting,
More blood will be spilled,
For . . . .
Silence no longer cries

## En-Masse

Like a thick blanket
Covering the moon,
Obscuring the light
Of the stars,
It is becoming increasingly difficult
To see any light
During these dark times

We struggle,
Rage and rale
Against the
Thoughts of others,
And the corporatocracy,
For we know
That delusion,
Preclusion,
Seclusion,
Exclusion and inclusion
Is the sign of the times

An ever-growing conundrum . . . of truth

Information,
Dis-information campaigns
Pains our spirits
For the need to know,
As words are freely sown
Amongst we,
The ignorant,
The unknowing.

News, fake
Is like
An old yeast,
It does not help the bread rise Momma,
It only is still yet
Unleavened . . . yet
We consume it
Just the same
In the name of 'Need'

The GMO seeds
Of malcontent
Have been planted
On good soil,
Bad soil,
And any other soil,
Mental, spiritual and otherwise . . .

And I ask,
"So what shall the harvest be?"

Will we ever see again,
Or will we forever have to peer
Through those kaleidoscopic lenses
Made just to upkeep
And maintain
The illusion . . .
…..
Confusion,
Yes,
Is this all but a test
To see who has the right
To cross-over
From this long night

# William S. Peters, Sr.

Unto a true Sun-Light
That is bright and clear
That has done away with fear
Of the out come ?

My penchant
To want to know
Is driving me looney,
Just like the toons
I used to watch
On the idiot box . . .

It worked I think,
For the ability
To distinguish
The various levels and dimensions
Of reality
Are slipping away . . .
En-masse

# June 2020 Featured Poets

~ * ~

Eftichia Kapardeli

Hussein Habasch

Kosh K Mathew

Metin Cengiz

# Eftichia Kapardeli

Kapardeli Eftichia has a Doctorate from ARTS and CULTURE WORLD ACADEMY She currently lives in Patras. She writes poetry, stories, short stories, hai-ku , essays. She studied journalism AKEM Has many awards in national competitions. Her work there is to many national and international anthologies.  She has a section at the University of Cyprus in Greek culture is a member of the world poets society. website is http://world-poets.blogspot. Com.  She is a member of the IWA (international writers and artists Association); chaired by Teresinka Pereira; had from IWA Certify 2017 as the best translation and  member of the POETAS DEL MUNDO .

kapardeli@gmail.com
https://www.facebook.com/PPdM.Mundial
https://twitter.com/Poetedumonde
http://eftichiakapa.blogspot.gr/2013_10_01_archive.html
http://isbn.nlg.gr/index.php?lvl=author_see&id=30410
https://www.facebook.com/kapardeli.eftichia
http://eftichiakapa.blogspot.gr/2013/08/blog-post_4143.html
http://worldpeaceacademy.blogspot.gr/2010/10/poets-for-world-peace.html

Eftichia Kapardeli

## ΤΟ ΘΑΥΜΑ

*Οι άνθρωποι της γενιάς μου
Ήχοι μοιάζουν πνιχτοί
Έτσι που διέσχισαν
Στην μέση της Ερήμου
Τις ζώνες του χρόνου
μόνοι και ξεχασμένοι*

*Λαβωμένοι, αθώοι αμνοί
Στην βοή της θυσίας
Με τα σημάδια στις πέτρες
από σώματα βασανισμένα, ζεστά και ολοζώντανα
σώματα τρυπημένα*

*Ο νέος άνεμος , μοίρασε τα ανυπεράσπιστα χέρια
τα άγρυπνα μάτια μας με ιαχές οδύνης
Στο θαύμα
Σμήνος μέλισσες ολότητες
της δοκιμασίας μας
της δύναμης της πίστης και της ελευθέριας μας*

## THE MIRACLE

The people of my generation
Sounds look like choked
So they crossed
In the middle of the desert
The time zones
alone and forgotten

Bloody, innocent lambs
In the roar of sacrifice
With the marks on the stones
from bodies tormented, hot and alive
bodies pierced

The new wind divorced the defenseless hands
our watchful eyes with screaming suffering
In the miracle
A bunch of bees , totals
of our test
the power of our faith and liberty

## ΜΥΣΤΙΚΟ ΖΩΗΣ

Το παγωμένο λουλούδι
τρύπησε την πέτρα
μοναχό
και εκεί αποκοιμήθη
Πέρασαν αιώνες
δακτύλιοι χρωμάτων
ξεδιπλώθηκαν και
θριάμβευσαν σαν
φωτός μεθη
\*\*\*
Με την ρίζα σφηνωμένη
στης ένωσης το
μέτρημα βαραίνει
τρυφερά γεννιέται και ανθεί πάλι
σε κρυφή αρμονία
το μυστικό της ζωής
Ξοδεύει

# SECRET LIFE

Ice flower
pierced the stone
alone and there dozing
They spent centuries
rings of color
unfolded and
they triumphed as
drunkenness light
\*\*\*
With the root
wedged of
the union
measuring weighs
the secret of life
spends in hidden harmony
tenderly born and flourishes again

Eftichia Kapardeli

## Η ΛΕΥΚΑ

Όταν ο Ήλιος από τις μεγάλες
αδιέξοδες νύχτες και τα μυστικά των αστεριών
ξεφεύγει και γλυκά ανατέλλει
μια γέρικη μοναχική Λεύκα
γεμίζει άστρα λευκά και με στερνά φιλιά
Βουλιάζει στο φως και μεθά

Τι κύκλος !!! μιας άγραφης συνθήκης
Το περίσσιο φως ανάσα μοιάζει της γης Θεάς


## An solitary poplar tree

When the Sun from the big ones
deadlocks nights and the secrets of the stars
escapes and sweetly rising
an old solitary poplar tree
it fills white stars and kisses
Dropping down to light and drunk

What circle !!! an unwritten treaty
breath looks like her
Earth goddess the overwhelming light

# Hussein Habasch

# Hussein Habasch

**Hussein Habasch:** He is a poet from *AFRIN/ KURDISTAN*, lives in Bonn-Germany.

Born in 1970. He writes in Kurdish and Arabic. Some of his poems were translated to manylanguages such as; English, German, Spanish, French, Chinese, Turkish, Persian, Albanian, Uzbek, Russian, Italian, Bulgarian, Lithuanian, Hungarian, Macedonian, Serbian and Romanian. A selection of his poems have been published in more than an international poetic anthology. He wrote these books: **Drowning in Roses**/ Azmina Publishing House, Amman, and Alwah Publishing House, Madrid 2002. **Fugitives across Ivros River**/ Sanabel Publishing House, Cairo 2004. **Higher than Desire and more Delicious than the Gazelle's Flank**/ Alwah Publishing House, Madrid 2007. **Delusions to Salim Barakat**/ Alzaman Publishing House, Damascus 2009. **A flying Angel (Texts about Syrian children)** Moment Publishing House, London 2013. **A flying Angel (Texts about Syrian children)** in English, Bogdani Publishing House 2015. **No pasarán**, in Spanish, the book published by the International Poetry Festival in Puerto Rico 2016. **Copaci Cu Chef**, in Romanian/ Ars Longa Publishing House, Bucharest 2017. **Dos Árboles**, in Spanish, the book published by the International Poetry Festival in El Salvador 2017. **Tiempos de Guerra**, in Spanish, the book published by the International Poetry Festival in Costa Rica 2017. **Fever of Quince**, in Kurdish/ Sersera Publishing House, Berlin 2019. **Peace for Afrin, peace for Kurdistan**, An international poetry anthology in English and Spanish/ Sersera Publishing House, Berlin 2019. **The red Snow**, in Chinese, published in Taiwan 2019.

# Hussein Habasch

## Snow Man

I give you a sweater,
Gloves,
A hat,
A coat,
And a vast field of snow.
Make a man from snow,
Put a carrot for nose,
Two cherries for eyes,
Your lipstick for mouth
Make the mouth smiles
Put the hat on
Wrap your shawl tenderly around his neck.
If you can't find him a name
Name him as mine.
Then gather the neighbourhood's kids
And tell them
That is my sweetheart
Come play with him!

*Translated by Muna Zinati*

## Five women in black scarves

Five women in black scarves
Lined up in front of missing people's desk!

The first said
I am looking for my husband's name
Missing two years ago.

The second said
I am looking for my son's name
Missing five years ago.

The third said
I am looking for my father's name
Missing four years ago.

The fourth said
I am looking for my sweetheart's name
Missing three years ago.

The fifth said
I am looking for my country's name
Missing hundreds of years ago!

The five women came out of the line
Crumbled on each other
As a tent, a horrible massacre happened upon it

And started the slapping and crying!

*Translated by Muna Zinati*

# The Lazy Pupil

They told him
Draw the school
He drew an amusement park.

Draw the teacher
He drew a rose.

Draw the lake
He drew a swan.

Draw Autumn
He drew a green bud.

Draw the sky
He drew his father.

Draw the earth
He drew his mother.

All the time
The lazy pupil
Was drawing his heart.

# Kosh K Mathew

# Kosh K Mathew

Dr.K.K.Mathew is a renowned physician and medical scientist of international repute. He is also a reputed poet and novelist. He has done many innovations in medical science, of which eight are first of its kind in medical science. He has published nine collection of English poems.

Website

www.mathewpakalomattam.org

# BLOOD

Me in the depth of despair, wrote on my heart
with the pencil so faint, that dim is my future
so hurtful, me see my name scribbled on my heart
the name fades with heavy rain that it is washed off
the heart weakens that it flutters to be written on
it with blood that oozed out, very beautiful the writing
that the blood sweetens my heart, it becomes rhythmic
the blood clotted on heart, inseparable that my name
engraved on me that nothing wiped it as it is blood-written,
not written by pencil which faded and the bond
unbreakable.

## THE RHYME

The solitude in me in rhythm, the rhythmic heart,
the rhythmic circulation of blood, respiration
in rhythm, intestines rhythmic, the man in rhythm,
with each rhythm, the rhyme of divinity comes out
rhymed by heart and soul, too faint to be picked
by the ears but internal senses grasp it, too sweet,
it condenses to honey that sweetens my heart
and soul, me absorbed in the divine chorus, sung
in the flow of love from Heaven to Earth, the solitude
filled with the murmur of flow that echoes in my heart.

## ABSORBED IN

The heart suffocates, the soul strangulated
me in despair, no fresh air to breathe, moon
peeps through the window, me alone in my
room, looked at the moon, my interior shakes
a moment, a new rhythm, new tune, rhyme
arises from my interior, spontaneously comes
out, sweet poem, me wrote long ago, it fills
every cell in me, that too jumps in exuberance
heart starts beating, arteries pulsates, brain
sharpened, the poem fills in me, each word
sweetens my soul, me absorbed in it for long
it dawned when me opened eyes, me energized.

# Metin Cengiz

# Metin Cengiz

Metin Cengiz: Poet and writer (b. 3 May 1953, Göle). He attended to Göle primary School (1964), Kars Alparslan High School (1972), and graduated from Erzurum Atatürk University, Faculty of Basic Sciences and Foreign Languages, Department of French Language and Literature (1977). When studying at the university he worked as a civil officer at the Turkish Statistical Institute for a short time (1973). In his youth he has been arrested many times for publishing political journals and engaging in political acts. He worked as a French language teacher between 1977-1987 in the provinces of Erzurum, Kars, and İstanbul. Meanwhile, he completed his studies at Marmara University, Department of French Language. He was sentenced for two years by the military government of 12 September 1980. During his service as a teacher he was exiled many times. Finally, when he was exiled to Muş, a rural province in the eastern Turkey, he resigned from civil service. He turned back to İstanbul and began to work as a proofreader, editor and translator at several publishing houses. In 1993 he returned to public service as a French language teacher and retired in 2002. […]

# Metin Cengiz

## ROSE

This well-shaped garden of you in my image
Like the past into which I couldn't go and come back
There it is always going to blossom like that

It is going to blossom in eternity
That garden in my image

*Translated by Müesser Yeniay*

## Night

Vibrant image of life, night
Spilling across the breadth of the earth
To its calm caressing flow, I have abandoned myself
In the wave where the stars fall to sleep
It scatters like gold dust
Tautens a chain of silver over the far shore

I reach my hand out to its face

The sun retreats yet again into the caves

*Translated by Neil P. Doherty*

## The Lamp

Still as a lake the scent of your body
So dense I am swimming through it

Its depth rising with the flickering of the flame
Its tongue like the swollen sea
At every stroke I come a little closer
At every stroke the lamp's shadow welcomes me

Sleep will not come, back and forth over
the sea of flickering flame thousands of stars trail
Round it the moon a tiny shadow
I must tread with caution, one could drown in the
Deeps

Carefully I reach out and dim the light
As though it were not me stretched out tired from head to
toe
But the lamp that drew Aladdin out of itself..


*Translated by Neil P. Doherty*

Metin Cengiz

# What Time Has Us Say

Like a snail,
On dry leaves leaving trails,
 Time slips through me

I have had my share of this world-
The sorrows that come with mud, pitch, and wave,
Leave no place for love.

What then I am the son of-
Around me like sand darkness abounds
And the sun and a desert of ice

The roof of words cracks
The mountains I entrusted collapse
As if I were a cavern made of doubt
The wind inside me howls.


*Translated by* Övünç Cengiz *and* Neil Patrick Doherty

# Remembering

our fallen soldiers of verse

*Janet Perkins Caldwell*
February 14, 1959 ~ September 20, 2016

*Alan W. Jankowski*
16 March 1961 ~ 10 March 2017

*Now available*
1 April 2020

World Healing World Peace
2020

Poets for Humanity

# Inner Child Press News

## Poetry Posse Members

## Inner Child Press News

We are so excited to share and announce a few of the current books, as well as the new and upcoming books of some of our Poetry Posse authors.

On the following pages we present to you ...

*Jackie Davis Allen*

*Gail Weston Shazor*

*hülya n. yılmaz*

*Nizar Sartawi*

*Faleeha Hassan*

*Fahredin Shehu*

*Caroline 'Ceri' Nazareno*

*Eliza Segiet*

*William S. Peters, Sr.*

The Year of the Poet VII ~ June 2020

## COMING SOON
www.innerchildpress.com

*Inner Child Press News*

**Now Available**
www.innerchildpress.com

The Year of the Poet VII ~ June 2020

## Now Available
### www.innerchildpress.com

*Inner Child Press News*

## COMING SOON

*www.innerchildpress.com*

The Book of krisar

volume v

william s. peters, sr.

The Year of the Poet VII ~ June 2020

## Now Available
### www.innerchildpress.com

# The Book of krisar

Volume I

william s. peters, sr.

# The Book of krisar

Volume II

william s. peters, sr.

*Inner Child Press News*

## Now Available
www.innerchildpress.com

# The Book of krisar
### Volume III

### william s. peters, sr.

# The Book of krisar
### Volume IV

### william s. peters, sr.

The Year of the Poet VII ~ June 2020

*Now Available*
www.innerchildpress.com

*Inner Child Press News*

**Now Available**
www.innerchildpress.com

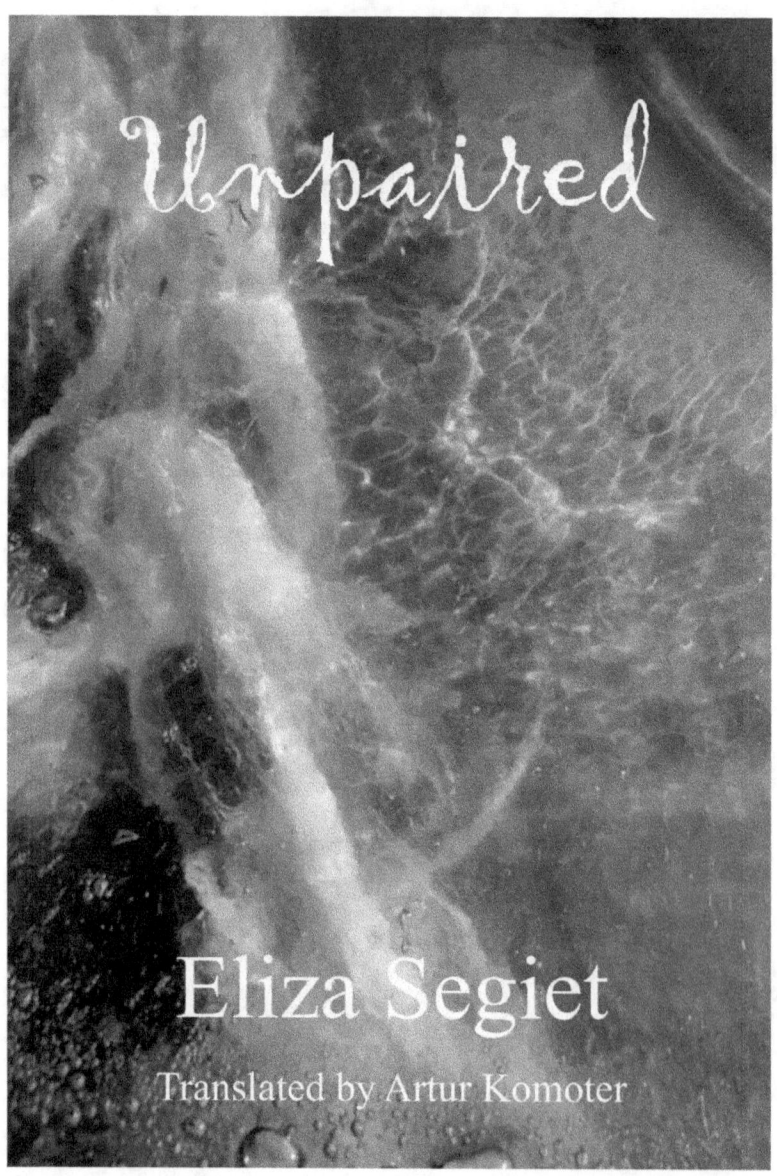

The Year of the Poet VII ~ June 2020

*Private Issue*
www.innerchildpress.com

*Inner Child Press News*

## Now Available
www.innerchildpress.com

The Year of the Poet VII ~ June 2020

Now Available at
www.innerchildpress.com

*Inner Child Press News*

## Now Available at
## www.innerchildpress.com

## The Year of the Poet VII ~ June 2020

### Now Available at
### www.innerchildpress.com

*Inner Child Press News*

**Now Available at**
www.innerchildpress.com

# HERENOW

FAHREDIN SHEHU

The Year of the Poet VII ~ June 2020

*Now Available at*
www.innerchildpress.com

*Inner Child Press News*

## Now Available at
### www.innerchildpress.com

The Year of the Poet VII ~ June 2020

Now Available at
www.innerchildpress.com

*Inner Child Press News*

## Now Available at
www.innerchildpress.com

The Year of the Poet VII ~ June 2020

Now Available at
www.innerchildpress.com

*Inner Child Press News*

## Now Available at
www.innerchildpress.com

The Year of the Poet VII ~ June 2020

**Now Available at**
www.innerchildpress.com

# Breakfast
for
# Butterflies

Faleeha Hassan

*Inner Child Press News*

**Now Available at**
www.innerchildpress.com

The Year of the Poet VII ~ June 2020

**Now Available at**
www.innerchildpress.com

*Inner Child Press News*

## Coming in the Summer of 2020

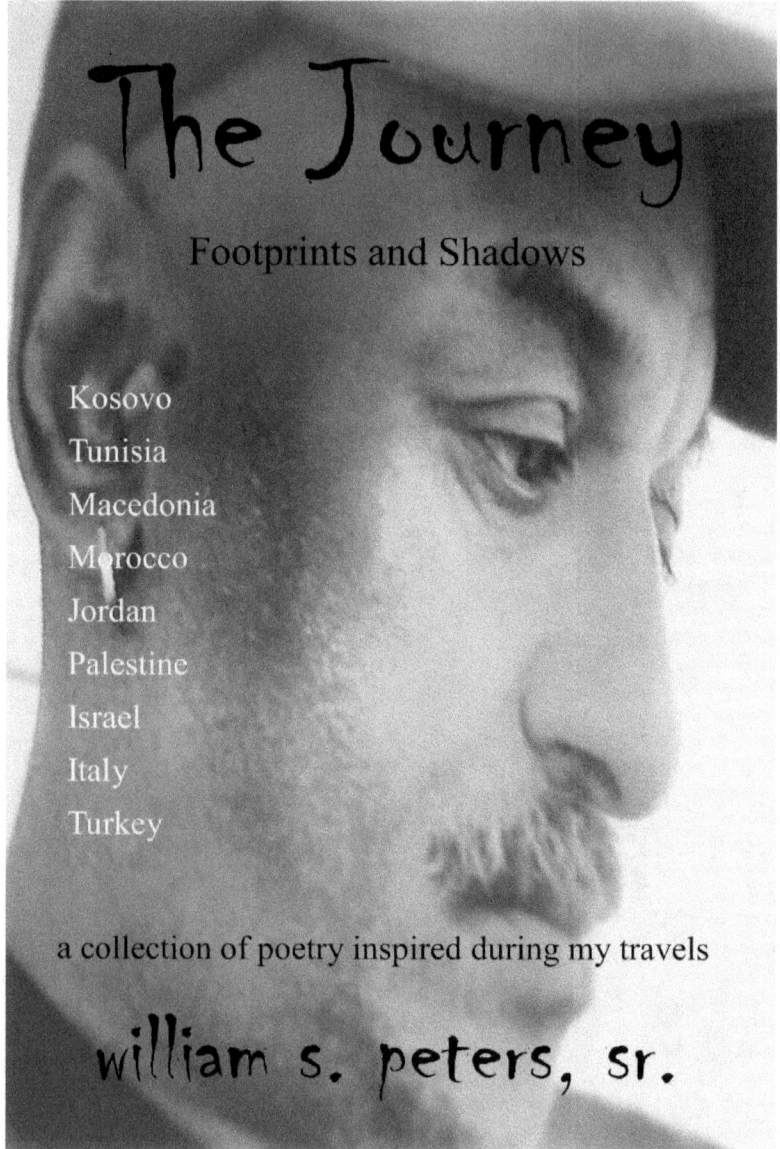

The Year of the Poet VII ~ June 2020

Now Available at
www.innerchildpress.com

*Inner Child Press News*

## Now Available at
## www.innerchildpress.com

Think on These Things
Book II

# william s. peters, sr.

# Other Anthological works from

Inner Child Press International

www.innerchildpress.com

*Inner Child Press Anthologies*

# World Healing World Peace
# 2020

## Poets for Humanity

*Now Available*

www.worldhealingworldpeacepoetry.com

Inner Child Press Anthologies

COMING SOON
www.innerchildpress.com

Inner Child Press Anthologies

the Heart of a Poet

words for a better tomorrow

The Conscious Poets

*COMING SOON*
*www.innerchildpress.com*

*Inner Child Press Anthologies*

*Now Available*
*www.innerchildpress.com*

Inner Child Press Anthologies

Now Available at
www.innerchildpress.com

Inner Child Press Anthologies

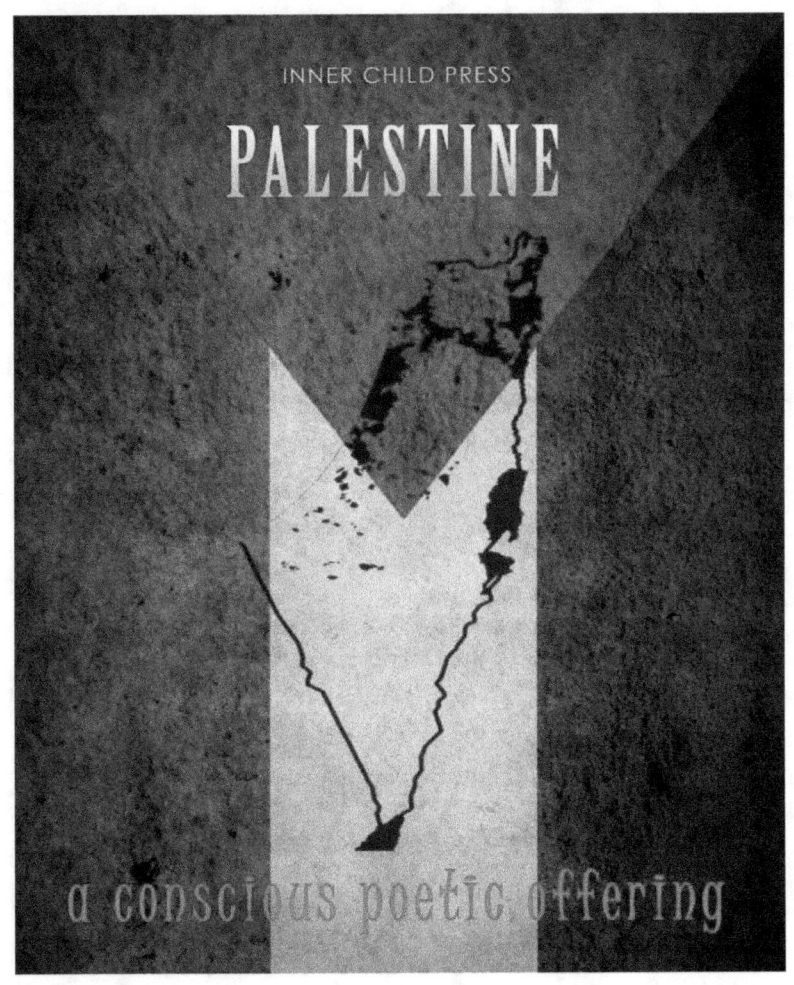

Now Available at
www.innerchildpress.com

*Inner Child Press Anthologies*

*Now Available at*
*www.innerchildpress.com*

Inner Child Press Anthologies

Now Available

www.worldhealingworldpeacepoetry.com

Inner Child Press Anthologies

Now Available

www.worldhealingworldpeacepoetry.com

## Inner Child Press Anthologies

### Now Available

www.worldhealingworldpeacepoetry.com

## Inner Child Press Anthologies

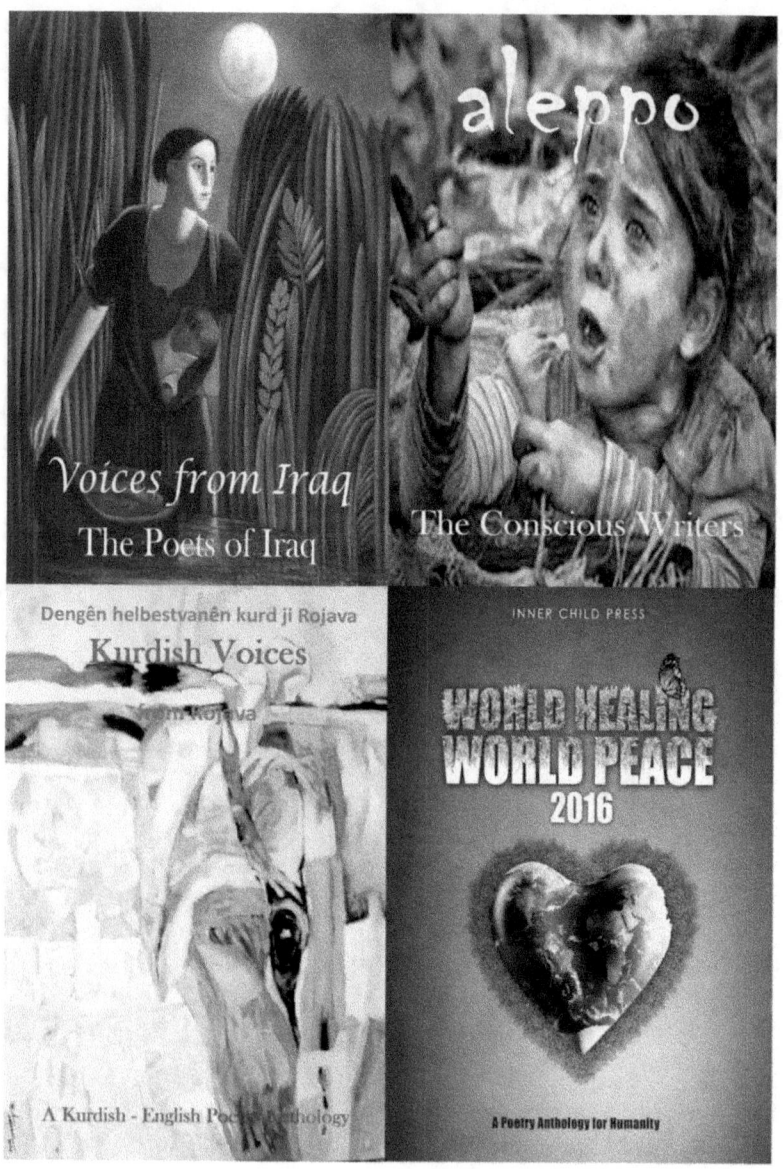

## Now Available

www.innerchildpress.com/anthologies

## Inner Child Press Anthologies

### Now Available

www.innerchildpress.com/anthologies

Inner Child Press Anthologies

Now Available

www.innerchildpress.com/anthologies

## Inner Child Press Anthologies

## Now Available

www.innerchildpress.com/anthologies

## Inner Child Press Anthologies

### Now Available

www.innerchildpress.com/anthologies

## Inner Child Press Anthologies

**Now Available**

www.innerchildpress.com/the-year-of-the-poet

## Inner Child Press Anthologies

### Now Available

www.innerchildpress.com/the-year-of-the-poet

## Inner Child Press Anthologies

### Now Available

www.innerchildpress.com/the-year-of-the-poet

## Inner Child Press Anthologies

## Now Available

www.innerchildpress.com/the-year-of-the-poet

## Inner Child Press Anthologies

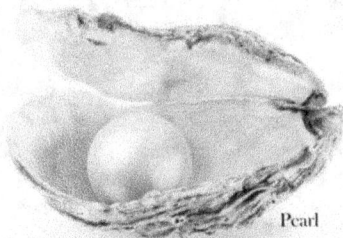

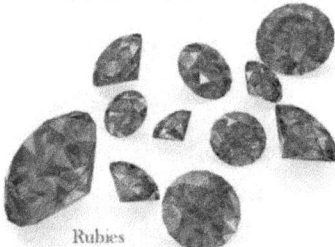

### Now Available

www.innerchildpress.com/the-year-of-the-poet

## Inner Child Press Anthologies

## Now Available

www.innerchildpress.com/the-year-of-the-poet

## Inner Child Press Anthologies

# Now Available

www.innerchildpress.com/the-year-of-the-poet

## Inner Child Press Anthologies

## Now Available

www.innerchildpress.com/the-year-of-the-poet

## Inner Child Press Anthologies

## Now Available

www.innerchildpress.com/the-year-of-the-poet

## Inner Child Press Anthologies

### Now Available

www.innerchildpress.com/the-year-of-the-poet

# Inner Child Press Anthologies

# Now Available

www.innerchildpress.com/the-year-of-the-poet

## Inner Child Press Anthologies

### The Year of the Poet IV
#### September 2017

**Featured Poets**
Martina Reisz Newberry
Ameer Nassir
Christine Fulco Neal
Robert Neal

The Elm Tree

**The Poetry Posse 2017**

Gail Weston Shazor * Caroline Nazareno * Bismay Mohanty
Teresa E. Gallion * Anna Jakubczak Vel Ratty Adalan
Joe DaVerbal Minddancer * Shareef Abdur – Rasheed
Albert Carrasco * Kimberly Burnham * Elizabeth Castillo
Hülya N. Yılmaz * Faleeha Hassan * Jackie Davis Allen
Jen Walls * Nizar Sartawi * * William S. Peters, Sr.

### The Year of the Poet IV
#### October 2017

**Featured Poets**
Ahmed Abu Saleem
Nedal Al-Qaeim
Sadeddin Shahin

The Black Walnut Tree

**The Poetry Posse 2017**

Gail Weston Shazor * Caroline Nazareno * Bismay Mohanty
Teresa E. Gallion * Anna Jakubczak Vel Ratty Adalan
Joe DaVerbal Minddancer * Shareef Abdur – Rasheed
Albert Carrasco * Kimberly Burnham * Elizabeth Castillo
Hülya N. Yılmaz * Faleeha Hassan * Jackie Davis Allen
Jen Walls * Nizar Sartawi * * William S. Peters, Sr.

### The Year of the Poet IV
#### November 2017

**Featured Poets**
Kay Peters
Alfreda D. Ghee
Gabriella Garofalo
Rosemary Cappello

The Tree of Life

**The Poetry Posse 2017**

Gail Weston Shazor * Caroline Nazareno * Bismay Mohanty
Teresa E. Gallion * Anna Jakubczak Vel Ratty Adalan
Joe DaVerbal Minddancer * Shareef Abdur – Rasheed
Albert Carrasco * Kimberly Burnham * Elizabeth Castillo
Hülya N. Yılmaz * Faleeha Hassan * Jackie Davis Allen
Jen Walls * Nizar Sartawi * William S. Peters, Sr.

### The Year of the Poet IV
#### December 2017

**Featured Poets**
Justice Clarke
Mariel M. Pabroa
Kiley Brown

The Fig Tree

**The Poetry Posse 2017**

Gail Weston Shazor * Caroline Nazareno * Bismay Mohanty
Teresa E. Gallion * Anna Jakubczak Vel Ratty Adalan
Joe DaVerbal Minddancer * Shareef Abdur – Rasheed
Albert Carrasco * Kimberly Burnham * Elizabeth Castillo
Hülya N. Yılmaz * Faleeha Hassan * Jackie Davis Allen
Jen Walls * Nizar Sartawi * William S. Peters, Sr.

### Now Available

www.innerchildpress.com/the-year-of-the-poet

## Inner Child Press Anthologies

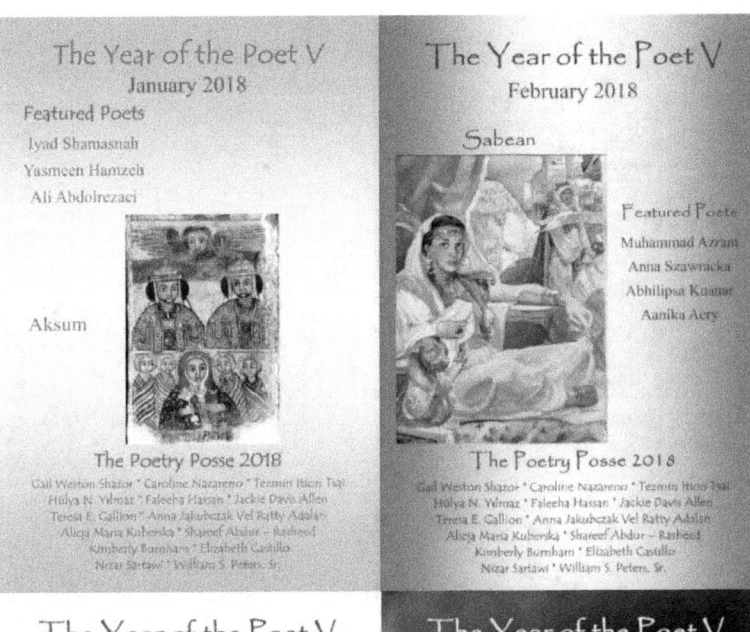

### Now Available

www.innerchildpress.com/the-year-of-the-poet

## Inner Child Press Anthologies

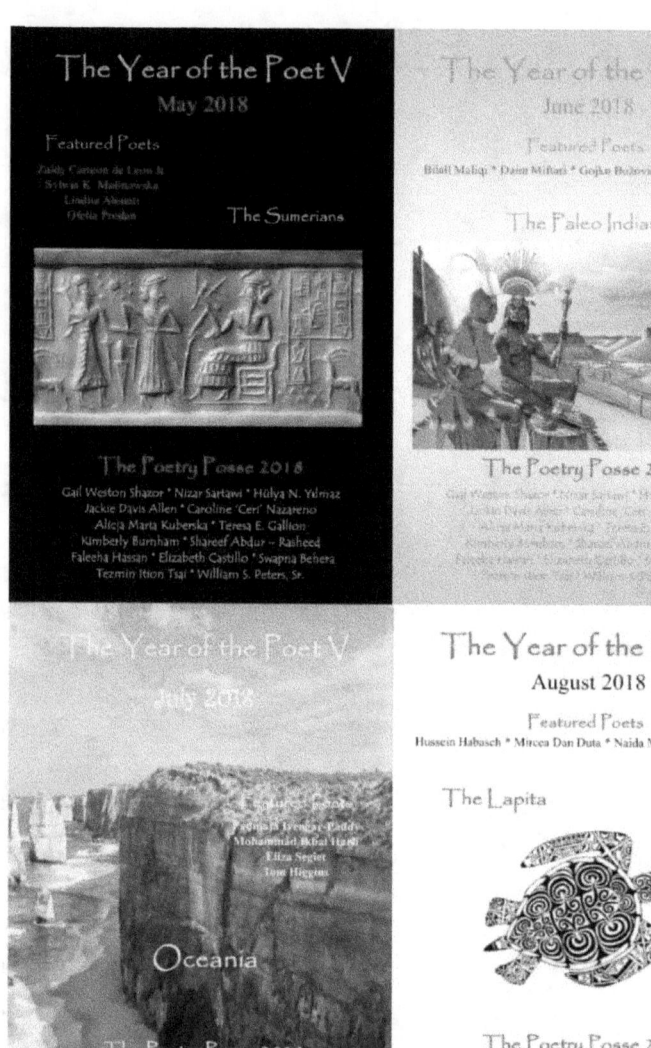

**Now Available**

www.innerchildpress.com/the-year-of-the-poet

# Inner Child Press Anthologies

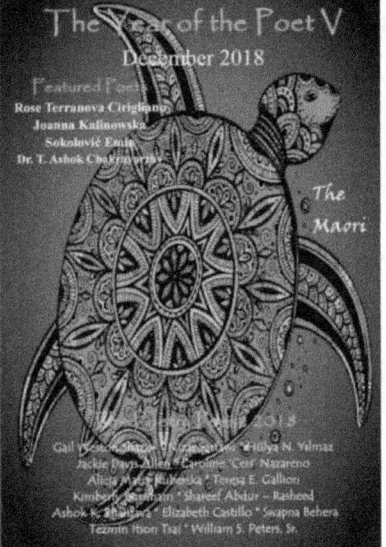

## Now Available

www.innerchildpress.com/the-year-of-the-poet

## Inner Child Press Anthologies

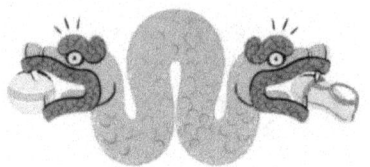

# Now Available

www.innerchildpress.com/the-year-of-the-poet

## Inner Child Press Anthologies

Now Available

www.innerchildpress.com/the-year-of-the-poet

## Inner Child Press Anthologies

### Now Available

www.innerchildpress.com/the-year-of-the-poet

Inner Child Press Anthologies

Now Available

www.innerchildpress.com/the-year-of-the-poet

*Inner Child Press Anthologies*

# The Year of the Poet VII
## May 2020

### Featured Poets
Alok Kumar Ray * Eden S. Trinidad
Franco Barbato * Izabela Zubko

### Ralph Bunche ~ 1950

The Year of Peace
Celebrating past Nobel Peace Prize Recipients

### The Poetry Posse 2020

Gail Weston Shazor * Albert Carassco * Hülya N. Yılmaz
Jackie Davis Allen * Caroline Nazareno * Eliza Segiet
Alicja Maria Kuberska * Teresa E. Gallion * Joe Paire
Kimberly Burnham * Shareef Abdur – Rasheed
Ashok K. Bhargava * Elizabeth Castillo * Swapna Behera
Tezmin Ition Tsai * William S. Peters, Sr.

*Now Available*

www.innerchildpress.com/the-year-of-the-poet

and there is much, much more !

visit . . .

www.innerchildpress.com/anthologies-sales-special.php

Also check out our Authors and all the wonderful Books Available at :

www.innerchildpress.com/authors-pages

# World Healing World Peace 2020

# Poets for Humanity

*Now Available*

www.worldhealingworldpeacepoetry.com

*Now Available*

www.worldhealingworldpeacepoetry.com

www.worldhealingworldpeacepoetry.com

# World Healing World Peace
## 2012, 2014, 2016, 2018, 2020

*Now Available*

www.worldhealingworldpeacepoetry.com

# Inner Child Press International

*'building bridges of cultural understanding'*

## Meet the Board of Directors

**William S. Peters, Sr.**
Chair Person
Founder
Inner Child Enterprises
Inner Child Press

**Hülya N Yılmaz**
Director
Editing Services
Co-Chair Person

**Fahredin B. Shehu**
Director
Cultural Affairs

**Elizabeth E. Castillo**
Director
Recording Secretary

**De'Andre Hawthorne**
Director
Performance Poetry

**Gail Weston Shazor**
Director
Anthologies

**Kimberly Burnham**
Director
Cultural Ambassador
Pacific Northwest
USA

**Ashok K. Bhargava**
Director
WIN Awards

**Deborah Smart**
Director
Publicity
Marketing

www.innerchildpress.com

# Inner Child Press International

*'building bridges of cultural understanding'*

## Meet our Cultural Ambassadors

Fahredin Shehu
Director of Cultural

Faleeha Hassan
Iraq ~ USA

Elizabeth E. Castillo
Philippines

Antoinette Coleman
Chicago
Midwest USA

Ananda Nepali
Nepal ~ Tibet
Northern India

Kimberly Burnham
Pacific Northwest
USA

Alicja Kuberska
Poland
Eastern Europe

Swapna Behera
India
Southeast Asia

Kolade O. Freedom
Nigeria
West Africa

Monsif Beroual
Morocco
Northern Africa

Ashok K. Bhargava
Canada

Tzemin Ition Tsai
Republic of China
Greater China

Alicia M. Ramirez
Mexico
Central America

Christena AV Williams
Jamaica
Caribbean

Louise Hudon
Eastern Canada

Aziz Mountassir
Morocco
Western Africa

Shareef Abdur-Rasheed
Southeastern USA

Laure Churazac
France
Western Europe

Mohammad Ikbal Harb
Lebanon
Middle East

Mohamed Abdel
Aziz Shmeis
Egypt
Middle East

Hilary Mainga
Kenya
Eastern Africa

Josephus R. Johnson
Liberia

## www.innerchildpress.com

This Anthological Publication
is underwritten solely by

*Inner Child Press International*

Inner Child Press is a Publishing Company Founded and Operated by Writers. Our personal publishing experiences provides us an intimate understanding of the sometimes daunting challenges Writers, New and Seasoned may face in the Business of Publishing and Marketing their Creative "Written Work".

For more Information

*Inner Child Press International*

www.innerchildpress.com

'building bridges of cultural understanding'
202 Wiltree Court, State College, Pennsylvania 16801

www.innerchildpress.com

*~ fini ~*

www.ingramcontent.com/pod-product-compliance
Lightning Source LLC
LaVergne TN
LVHW022322080426
835508LV00041B/1747